W9-CHL-871

HERITAGE
AN AFRICAN-AMERICAN
QUOTE BOOK

HERITAGE

AN AFRICAN-AMERICAN

QUOTE BOOK

EDITED BY SUSAN CARNAHAN

ARIEL BOOKS

ANDREWS AND MCMEEL
KANSAS CITY

Book design by Diane Stevenson of Snap-Haus Graphics

Photographs on pp. 6, 23, 24, 27, 30, and 37 copyright © 1994 by Bruce Caines; all other photographs from UPI/Corbis-Bettmann

ISBN: 0-8362-1526-5

CONTENTS

INTRODUCTION

If now isn't a good time for the truth I don't see when we'll get to it.

—NIKKI GIOVANNI

The words of wise people have always had the power to encourage and inspire, to clarify and instruct. In any decade and for any group of people, inherited wisdom is a rich source of community strength, the birthplace of self-reliance and self-esteem. The most successful leaders—political, spiritual, cultural—are those who have learned to draw upon this heritage of thought and experience.

PHADREA PONDS
NATURAL-RESOURCE BIOLOGIST

Gathered in this volume are the insightful sayings of black people from around the world, talking about role models, personal responsibility, culture and community, and the struggle for equality. They are the voices of men and women, artists and athletes, spokespersons and scholars. Resonant with history, they are illuminating and cautionary, funny and sincere. They speak primarily for the African-American community, but the wisdom they impart is timeless and speaks to us all, regardless of race or ancestry.

The African-American community maintains its cultural independence and solid partnership with the world around it through a strength of vision that withstands the vagaries of political and social change. As a transcript of cultural understanding, this book helps to nourish and keep that vision alive. Read it for inspiration, for enjoyment, and for appreciation of clear-eyed wisdom that has passed from generation to generation.

Champions aren't made in gyms. Champions are made from something they have deep inside them—a desire, a dream, a vision. They have to have last-minute stamina, they have to be a little faster, they have to have the skill, and the will. But the will must be stronger than the skill.

—Muhammad Ali

MODELS

OF

EXCELLENCE

Black minds and talent have skills to control a spacecraft or scalpel with the same finesse and dexterity with which they control a basketball.

—RONALD MCNAIR

A white child might need a role model, but a black child needs more than that in this society. He needs hope.

—HANK AARON

CARL LEWIS
OLYMPIC MEDALIST

For every one of us that succeeds, it's because there's somebody there to show you the way out. The light doesn't necessarily have to be in your family; for me it was teachers and school.

—OPRAH WINFREY

There are no secrets to success: Don't waste time looking for them. Success is the result of perfection, hard work, learning from failure, loyalty to those for whom you work, and persistence.

—COLIN POWELL

I had to make my own living and my own opportunity. . . . Don't sit down and wait for the opportunities to come; you have to get up and make them.

—MADAME C. J. WALKER

TONI MCINTOSH
PITTSBURGH'S FIRST FEMALE FIREFIGHTER

Momma . . . rose alone to apocalyptic silence, set the sun in our windows, and daily mended the world.

—PAULETTE CHILDRESS WHITE

I have discovered in life that there are ways of getting almost anywhere you want to go, if you really want to go.

—LANGSTON HUGHES

Nothing ever comes to one, that is worth having, except as a result of hard work.

—BOOKER T. WASHINGTON

I was raised to believe that excellence is the best deterrent to racism or sexism. And that's how I operate my life.

—OPRAH WINFREY

Excellence is the name of the game no matter what color or what country you're from. If you are the best at what you're doing, then you have my admiration and respect.

—JUDITH JAMISON

EUBIE BLAKE
JAZZ PIANIST

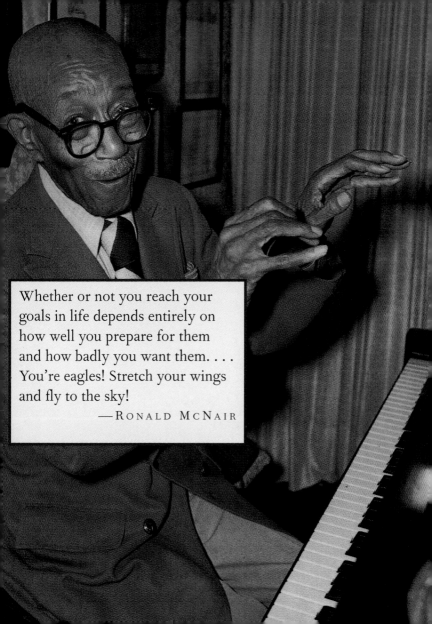

Whether or not you reach your goals in life depends entirely on how well you prepare for them and how badly you want them. . . . You're eagles! Stretch your wings and fly to the sky!

—RONALD MCNAIR

I make an active effort to remain a positive role model to kids. They need people to show them there's another way.

—M. C. HAMMER

I don't believe in luck. . . . It's persistence, hard work, and not forgetting your dream.

—JANET JACKSON

Throughout all her bitter years of slavery [my mother] managed to preserve a queenlike dignity.

—MARY MCLEOD BETHUNE

Because I want every kid to be viewed as a person rather than as a member of a certain race does not mean that I'm not black enough. . . . Do they want me to be positive just for black kids and negative for everybody else?

—MICHAEL JORDAN

Role model? My mother leads the pack. . . . I regard her as I do all of the other black women throughout history: miraculous.

—CICELY TYSON

The black athlete carries the image of the black community. He carries the cross, in a way, until blacks make inroads in other dimensions.

—ARTHUR ASHE

I have no Messiah complex and I know that we may need many leaders to do the job. . . . Let us not succumb to divisions and conflicts. The job ahead is too great.

—MARTIN LUTHER KING JR.

I made the most of my ability and I did my best with my title.

—JOE LOUIS

I don't think a person has to use drugs [to excel in athletics]. There is no substitute for hard work.

—FLORENCE GRIFFITH-JOYNER

What you want to defeat is the idea that says your individuality doesn't count—that all you are is black. You want to say, "But I'm a person. Not a political entity."

—JAMAICA KINCAID

It is critical that we take charge of our own destiny and stop waiting for some unknown mythical being to come along and wipe racism from the face of this earth.

—DAVID C. WILSON

I thought I could change the world. It took me a hundred years to figure out I can't change the world. I can only change Bessie. And honey, that ain't easy either.

—BESSIE DELANY

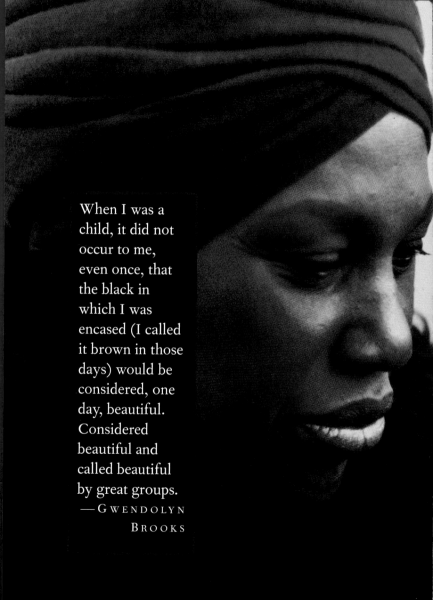

When I was a
child, it did not
occur to me,
even once, that
the black in
which I was
encased (I called
it brown in those
days) would be
considered, one
day, beautiful.
Considered
beautiful and
called beautiful
by great groups.
— GWENDOLYN
    BROOKS

HERITAGE AND IDENTITY

I believe in pride of race and lineage and self: in pride of self so deep as to scorn injustice to other selves. Especially do I believe in the Negro Race: in the beauty of its genius, the sweetness of its soul, and its strength in that meekness which shall yet inherit this turbulent earth.

—W. E. B. DuBois

We need to haunt the halls of history and listen anew to the ancestors' wisdom.

—Maya Angelou

Leontyne Price
OPERA SINGER

HERITAGE

You must understand, being Black is more involved than just wearing an X cap. It means being committed to furthering our race and nurturing our children. Being Black runs deeper than just having rhythm. It means possessing a history of more than three hundred years of fighting for freedom and equality.

—ELIZABETH RIDLEY

It's not a ladder we're climbing, it's literature we're producing. . . . We cannot possibly leave it to history as a discipline nor to sociology nor science nor economics to tell the story of our people.

—NIKKI GIOVANNI

I don't sing a song unless I feel it. The song don't tug at my heart, I pass on it. I have to believe in what I'm doing.

—RAY CHARLES

WALLACE HILL AND ANDY HILL (HUSBAND AND WIFE

America is woven of many strands; I would recognize them and let it so remain. . . . Our fate is to become one, and yet many. This is not prophecy, but description.

—RALPH ELLISON

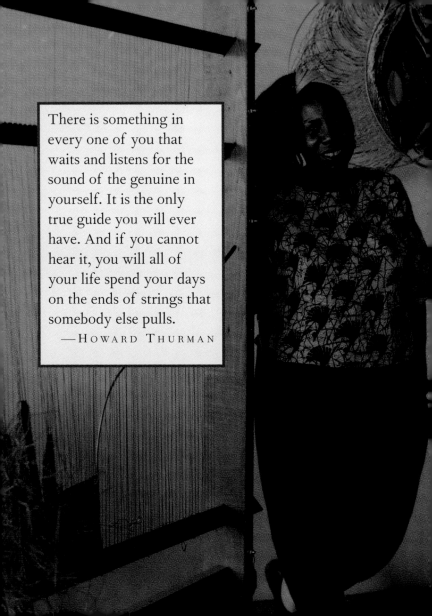

There is something in
every one of you that
waits and listens for the
sound of the genuine in
yourself. It is the only
true guide you will ever
have. And if you cannot
hear it, you will all of
your life spend your days
on the ends of strings that
somebody else pulls.
——HOWARD THURMAN

Parents have become so convinced that educators know what is best for children that they forget that they themselves are really the experts.

—MARIAN WRIGHT EDELMAN

The genius of our black foremothers and forefathers was . . . to equip black folk with cultural armor to beat back the demons of hopelessness, meaninglessness, and lovelessness.

—CORNEL WEST

Guided by my heritage of a love of beauty and a respect for strength—in search of my mother's garden I found my own.

—ALICE WALKER

My blackness has never been in my hair. Blackness is not a hairstyle.

—BERTHA K. GILKEY

We wanted something for ourselves and for our children, so we took a chance with our lives.

—UNITA BLACKWELL

There were times when we were broke and I knew it. Dad found a way to sacrifice a quarter for me. I must keep that natural circle of love going around for my own son.

—GREGORY HINES

I never considered my race as a barrier to me. In fact, it's become an asset because it allows me to have a broader perspective.

—JAMES G. KAISER

As African-Americans, we must continue to instill in our children a desire to actively participate in the economic development of the black community. . . .

—EARL GRAVES

BRANFORD MARSALIS
JAZZ SAXOPHONIST

I've always told
the musicians in
my band to play
with what they
know and then
play *above that*.
Because then any-
thing can happen,
and that's where
great art and
music happens.
—MILES DAVIS

We are the one race of women who could offer such seemingly disparate styles as Rosa Parks's and Billie Holiday's as perfect examples of who we are, and find a little bit of them in each of us.

—BONNIE ALLEN

Schooling is what happens inside the walls of the school, some of which is educational. Education happens everywhere, and it happens from the moment a child is born—and some people say before—until it dies.

—SARA LAWRENCE LIGHTFOOT

Two parents can't raise a child any more than one. You need a whole community—everybody—to raise a child.

—TONI MORRISON

A man without ambition is dead. A man with ambition but no love is dead. A man with ambition and love for his blessings here on earth is ever so alive.

—PEARL BAILEY

Would America have been America without her Negro people?

—W. E. B. DuBois

My father, with only a second-grade education, was the hardest working man I ever knew. I think I got most of my drive from him.

—JAMES BROWN

In my world, black women
can do anything.
—JULIE DASH

Let the Afro-American depend on no party, but on himself for his salvation.

—IDA B. WELLS

I had a heritage, rich and nearer than the tongue which gave it voice. My mind resounded with the words and my blood raced to the rhythms.

—MAYA ANGELOU

We're a great heart people.

—PEARL BAILEY

BARBARA BRANDON

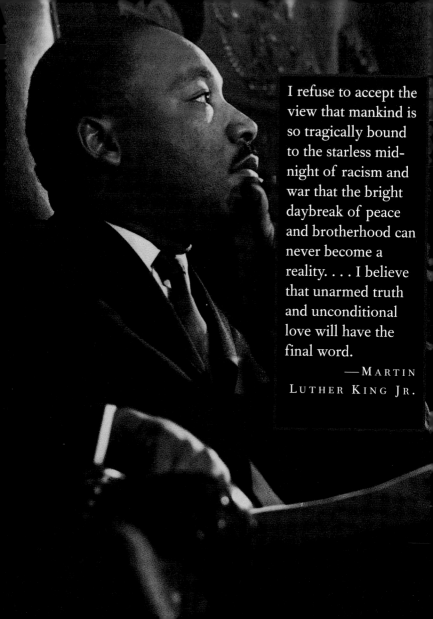

I refuse to accept the view that mankind is so tragically bound to the starless midnight of racism and war that the bright daybreak of peace and brotherhood can never become a reality. . . . I believe that unarmed truth and unconditional love will have the final word.

—MARTIN LUTHER KING JR.

NO EASY WALK

The need for change bulldozed a road down the center of my mind.

—MAYA ANGELOU

There was only one thing I could do—hammer relentlessly, continually crying aloud, even if in a wilderness, and force open, by sheer muscle power, every closed door.

—ADAM CLAYTON POWELL JR.

A man must be willing to die for justice. Death is an inescapable reality and men die daily, but good deeds live forever.

—REV. JESSE JACKSON

MARTIN LUTHER KING JR.
CIVIL RIGHTS LEADER

HERITAGE

I started with this idea in my head, "There's two things I've got a right to, death or liberty."

—HARRIET TUBMAN

If there is no struggle, there is no progress.

—FREDERICK DOUGLASS

Education is the primary tool of emancipation and liberation for African-Americans in our fight for true equality in this country.

—EARL G. GRAVES

Brotherhood is a two-way street.

—MALCOLM X

In every human breast, God has implanted a principle which we call love of freedom; it is impatient of oppression and pants for deliverance.

—PHILLIS WHEATLEY

SHIRLEY CHISHOLM

When people made up their minds that they wanted to be free and took action, then there was a change.

—ROSA PARKS

HERITAGE

Those who profess to favor freedom, and yet deprecate agitation, are men who want crops without plowing up the ground.

—FREDERICK DOUGLASS

Once you begin to explain or excuse all events on racial grounds, you begin to indulge in the perilous mythology of race. It is dangerous to say 'the white man is the cause of my problems' or 'the black man is the cause of my problem . . .' substitute any color—the danger is implicit.

—JAMES EARL JONES

The cost of liberty is less than the price of repression.

—W. E. B. DUBOIS

There will always be some curve balls in your life.
Teach your children to thrive in that adversity.

—JEANNE MOUTOUSSAMY-ASHE

The American Negro believes in democracy. We want to make it real, complete, workable, not only for ourselves—the thirteen million dark ones—but for all Americans all over the land.

—LANGSTON HUGHES

No person is your friend who demands your silence, or denies your right to grow.

—ALICE WALKER

A man who won't die for something is not fit to live.

—MARTIN LUTHER KING JR.

We must turn to each other and not on each other.

—REV. JESSE JACKSON

The destiny of the colored American . . . is the destiny of America.

—FREDERICK DOUGLASS

There is no easy walk to freedom anywhere and many of us will have to pass through the valley of the shadow of death again and again before we reach the mountaintop of our desires.

—NELSON MANDELA

In every crisis there is a message. Crises are nature's way of forcing change—breaking down old structures, shaking loose negative habits so that something new and better can take their place.

—SUSAN L. TAYLOR

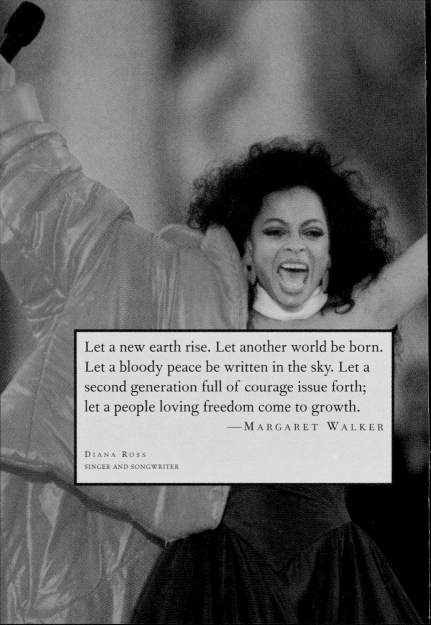

Let a new earth rise. Let another world be born.
Let a bloody peace be written in the sky. Let a
second generation full of courage issue forth;
let a people loving freedom come to growth.
——Margaret Walker

Diana Ross
singer and songwriter